# RUSTY GALLOWS

# PASSAGES AGAINST HATE

VAGABOND
VENICE/CULVER CITY, CA

# RUSTY GALLOWS

## PASSAGES AGAINST HATE

## Dee Allen.

VAGABOND

editor@vagabondbooks.net

Published by VAGABOND
Mark Lipman, editor

VAGABOND

Intellectual Property
Allen., Dee
Rusty Gallows
1st ed. / p.cm.

ISBN13: 978-1-936293-47-6

Made in the USA.

The Hanging Bridge – Shubuta, Mississippi – Circa 1966

# TABLE OF CONTENTS

*for J.D.*

[ Jeanette Desboine ]

*To ignore evil is to become an accomplice to it.*
Rev. Martin Luther King, Junior

# DOCTRINE

From the oldest living generation
To the youngest
It is taught.
Passed down
Like a hereditary disease.
Mind-killing
Heart-infecting pathogen
Which, in turn,
Infects sentences, whole conversations
So much it dominates voice & emotion.

"If you're not Christian,
You are the enemy."
"If you're not Black,
You are the enemy."
These were the lessons
I learned in pieces
From knee-high to a roach
To all grown up,
From my relatives' chosen
Words and actions.

The door stays closed
If you're the wrong colour.
Anyone who doesn't
Look like you shouldn't be trusted.
Especially if they
Have blue eyes & fair skin.
The other name for "opponent"
Is "White" in most of my family.

Yesterday's victims
Are today's carriers
Of race hate.
Their doctrine, ethnic self-defense.
Like a hereditary disease,
Passed down.
It is taught
To the youngest
From the oldest living generation.

W: 6.30.08  REV: 4.19.2020

# WITHOUT TEETH

Forty-two years ago,
His precious life
Was snatched from us.
The will of assassins:
Inert Black flesh.

A sudden rifle-blast
Ripped through the early April Memphis morning,
Then through him,
"The peacemaker."

A world based on total equality
Remained a dream
In stillbirth.
His life stolen
By parties unknown,
Given to the dark abyss,
His body, given to the cold ground.
His dream

Left unknown
Generations thereafter.

Forty-two years later,
The pin drop
Is the only sound heard over an
Enveloping silence.
No one really mourns for him.
No acknowledgement of his untimely demise.
His life's work, done in vain.

Candles aren't lit
For the son of Atlanta's soil.
Activists have given the integrationist of yore
The collective brush-off.
A national holiday commemorating
His birth occurs every January and it's
Another day off from
Slaving away for teachers & bosses.

Yes, he's been to the mountaintop without us.
Yes, he's had a dream

And yet

No one knows what that dream was
Or for whom.

The sum of his achievements
On this earthly plane
Reduced to
Four or five
Simple words
Two phrases
Carrying little meaning to the average person
Now.

"I HAVE A DREAM."
"I'VE BEEN TO THE MOUNTAINTOP."

His other traits are clearly forgotten,
Lost in the dissonance
Of those same
Four or five words
Repeated like some holy mantra
In most minds of this generation:

Anti-war
Anti-imperialist
Pro-worker
Poverty's
Enemy
Third World
Insurrection's
Advocate
Mouthpiece
Against this Western Empire.

That man is never spoken of –
In Establishment circles.

That man was neutralized
Before his work could take fruition.
That Georgia preacher's son
Would have fought back, if tested hard enough.
Liberals,
Conservatives,

White Christians,
Corporations
Praising to the sky
"The peacemaker" today
Would've called him
"Troublemaker" yesterday.

So much easier to give accolades to a man of peace
Long after he's dead –

Accolades
To the great 20th Century Black Christian
Myth
Of a saint,
A non-violent man,

A once-living dream of racial tolerance,
A leader who ignored internecine wars elsewhere.

An Amerikkkan Black hero
Without teeth.

Safe in contrast
To other Black heroes of the past,
Starting with the shrewd inciters of
Slave revolts from Ghana to Ayiti* to
The Amistad, continuing through
Today's political prisoners
And voices of the unheard
In city riots. But he's no less important to my people's
                        history of survival.

In 1965,
While standing in the middle of
Scorched, riot-torn Watts,
That Georgia preacher's son
Who experienced a sharp, radical turn
In his outlook that reflected
His last three years

Is now
Softer & sanitised for everyone's protection.
A beloved Amerikkkan Black hero
Without teeth. No longer a threat.

No one

That is,

No one
Who dares to pick up a book
Can separate the man from the cherished
Public myth.
Forever behind the pulpit in Washington D.C.
Addressing anti-racist thousands
In a wide field of picket signs & banners.
Perpetual paragon of civil rights
And only civil rights.

---

W: Hurricane Katrina Anniversary 2010

*The Kreyol-language name for Haiti.

# SCRATCH

Amidst these days of disaster & fright,
We've seen the emergence of the Alt-Right,
Flocking to street protests like hungry vultures
Out of fear of losing vicious Southern White culture.

Hatred wears a whole other face –
Just scratch beneath the civil carapace,
With friendly eyes & grinning lips.
Under digging nails, the charade won't persist.

Flakes fall to the floor, your mouth decries
The look of the ally before your eyes,
With frowning mouth & disdainful scowl,
Cursing your kind with words most foul.

The truth stands in front, shatters perception.
"Good intentioned comrade," convenient deception.
And truth provokes thought, none left safest:
*Scratch a liberal, find a racist.*\*

---

W: 11.3.17

\*End-quote from Oakland poet Mark G.

# BLOOD AND SOIL

WHOSE BLOOD
     WHOSE SOIL
         Does the raging
            Neo-Nazi shout for?

THE BLOOD –
    European stock
        One hundred percent
           Free from perceived
              Blemish from other kinds.

THE SOIL –
    The land
        The fair of skin
           Feel entitled to work
            & dominate.

           Territoriality's heart-felt demand.

THE BLOOD –
    Indigenous stock
        Shed in holocausts
           Settler armies started
             & haters want continued.

THE SOIL –
    The continent
        Snatched from under
           Red feet, Black hands
              Built & driven the realm excluding them
                  still.

           Colonialism's raw-throat cry.

ANGRY WHITE MEN
    Torches in fists
        March the road
           At night declaring
            No removal
              Of their ancient idols
                Of INTIMIDATION
                  PASSED DOWN –

For the belligerent
    For the ignorant
        Prejudice
            Has a rallying cry –

---

W: 11.15.17

# ALL LIVES MATTER

in conversational form
really means

I DON'T WANNA
TALK ABOUT RACE
AT ANY TIME!
NOW
SHUT THE HELL UP!

---

W: 11.19.17

# WESTERN CHAUVINIST

All constant denial
Of Fascist ways and pushing
White dopes into kick-
Starting fights with the non-White
Folks makes Gavin a proud boy.

---

W: Ramadan 2020
[ For Gavin McInnes. ]

# RED & BLACK

Your reason for existence:
Manufacture fear with racial slurs
Our reason for existence:
Ridding the land of the Fascist Curse

Your expressions of pride
Usually lead to genocide
No matter where your numbers abide
Expect black boots up in your backside

Coming out to terrorize
Far Right movement leeches
You'll never give anyone freedom
So we'll shut down your venomous speeches

Your preachings lack
Parity and tact
Your faces, our fists make contact

When coming up against the red & black

The wind of change
Has a powerful gust
More of you,
More of us

Your degenerate
Dream of race war
Comes to an end when
You hit the fucking floor

Let every separatist
Snowflake understand
All colors & creeds
Are welcome in our land

You won't get
One inch, not a single tract
Know lessons in
Pain from the red & black.

W: 6.8.18

# CONCRETE ALTAR

Black lives
Don't matter
To the C.O.*
Walking the cell-block.

Black lives
Matter less
To the salty
Beat-cop patrolling the 'hood, squadcar on prowl.

Black lives
Don't matter
To the vigilante
Bigot gone hunting for heads darker than his.

Black lives

Matter less
To sharp steel
Unprovoked

Insane wrath thrust
Into young
Necks on
A subway train platform.

One female left wounded. Her sister
Never saw past 18.

MacArthur B.A.R.T.**
Past sundown:
Gleaming candles, flowers & photos,
Altar formed over concrete.
People, victim's family gathered
Among blaring Hip Hop tracks
And wall projections of

Light-skinned Nia
In happier times, the
Look of another adolescent
In love
With life

Demanded a justice for her
None of them knew.
Protect your necks.
Protect each other,
Little sisters
And brothers.

---

W: 7.24.18
[ For Nia Wilson – 2000 – 2018. ]

* Correctional Officer. Another name for "prison guard."
** Bay Area Rapid Transit.

# SHORN

Getting the head
Shorn with a blade,
Hairless to the touch
And smooth, was how
Kenyan and Tanzanian
Maasai men historically
Prepared for battle
Against approaching hostile
Nearby tribes. Nowadays,
Maasai women strip
Themselves of wooly hair
For cleanliness and
Drawing the straying
Male eye on them –
As an African man

In America, applying
A good razor
To my stubbly
Scalp, lathered in
Thick white cream,
Backward and forward
In the bathroom mirror
Over a face-bowl

Keeps the creeping
Ravages of grey
From settling in
All too soon –

My face,
All sharp corners
And high cheek-bones,
Receives the same treatment.

My ritual
Wards off age
For the time being.
Youth and
Cleanliness maintained by razor strokes.

This is me
In warrior mode
Preparing for battle
Against encroaching hostile
Western society.

---

W: 8.16.18

The Hanging Bridge – Shubuta, Mississippi – Circa 1942

# Rusty Gallows

Reddish-brown
Corrosion covers
The whole goddamn structure
Like a filthy blanket.
With so much widespread
Decay, this old
Tarnished bridge should have
Collapsed from crashing waters
Many floods ago,
By some fluke of nature,
Unscathed by time, it still
Stands above the muddy
Chickasawhay River in
Shubuta, Mississippi.

Once a passageway to a long
Forgotten Clarke County destination,
Twice an implement
Of execution
Like an iron crucifix.

THIS IS YOU
Skull and crossbones

Etched on the bridge's base
Cryptic warning
Meant for anyone
Unlucky enough to cross it
And the invisible line
Away from "their place."

Between both world wars,
Unspecified parties –
Let's re-phrase that –
Haters strung up
Four boys,
Two girls
Both pregnant,
Young, Negro and
Guilty of nothing
Hung from knotted ropes
Tied to rusty girders

Over the coursing river
Like six
Black flags
Sailing in
The gentle
Southern wind.

W: 8.17.18
[ Inspired by the book *Hanging Bridge* by Jason Morgan Ward. ]

The Hanging Bridge – Shubuta, Mississippi – Today

Jackson Advocate, 1942

**AMAGES**

ecklessly
an em-
seriously
d a suit
esterday
her hus-
ates that
ke a ride
g in Fos-
towship,
ankment
her hus-
result of

the party which permits such injustice to continue would be driven from power.

# FOUR NEGROES LYNCHED

MOBILE, ALA., Dec. 20.—(A. P.)— Four Negroes, two of them women, accused of the murder of Dr. E. L. Johnson here last week, were taken from the jail at Shubuta, Miss., tonight and lynched, according to information received in Mobile. All four are reported to have been hanged to the girders of a bridge spanning the Chickasahay River.

Pittsburgh Post-Gazette, 1918

# Crann Tara*

It was a religious symbol

Epitomising Nazarene
Saviour's grace
Fashioned from
Rope and
Two sticks
And set
Burning to
A crisp

That caught
Painted-faced,
Kilt-wearing
Clansmen's attention.
Hallowed flame
Inspired them
To raise
Shields and
Sharp swords
Upon other
Clans, demonstrated
Supremacy over
Medieval Scottish
Highland hills.

Holy emblem
On fire
Equals
Battle
Signal.

It was a religious symbol

Blazing hot
Celtic rite
Resurrected for
The flickering
Silent movie
Big screen
In 1915.
D.W. Griffith

Unveiled his
Box-office hit
Featuring Black
Brute-hunting
Klansmen on
Covered horses.
Reconstruction Era's
Inversion vile
Where the
Enslaving South
Rose again
As heroic.
Supremacist twist

That caught
Small-minded,
Race-fearing
White's attention.
Desecrated cross
Inspired them
To revive
From death
An invisible
Empire sworn
To create
Nightly terror,
Amplified hate
And massive
Street presence.

Holy emblem
On fire
United
Total
Scum

And planted
Fright into
The heart
The way

Police squad car
Sirens can

For us
Non-Whites now.

---

W: 8.22.18

* Scottish Gaelic: "Fiery cross."

# Unholy Beast

Tempestuous rainy night
Brightened by lightning flash –
Streak of electricity
Strikes iron rod wrapped with wires –

Raw electricity travels via
Wires connected to the laboratory
Subject supine under white sheet, over
Operating table, gasping, twitching to life

For an instant, just to die.
The scientist watches his invention,
Surgery by-product, human death stitched to human death,
Reawaken, walk to him as he recoils in horror at what he'd made –

This is a two-hundred year-old
Story everybody knows, even to those
Who never read books
Or watch Horror films.

The United States
In Century 21
Has an unholy beast
On the loose all its own

Spreading terror to all
In his path or not,
Only this one's
Not a patchwork being

And he's armed.
Three Glocks and an AR-15 deliver
His animalistic rage to all quarters.

Mary Shelley's legendary, literary hulk and him

Share common footing
In one area:

Both beasts are
Controlled by hatred.

Caravans of Honduran
Migrants, on foot headed for the dream-asylum
Here, *El Norté,* and their American allies' embrace –

Roots of his violent scorn easily inform

Snap decision to lock, load and take aim
At his
Personal
Geneva:

Tree Of Life
Synagogue,
Pittsburgh.
The result:

Eleven
Confirmed kills of
Eleven
Confirmed Jews.

Work of a monster.

---

W: 11.3.18

# THE MYSTERY ENDS

Slavery
Kept us
Ignorant and confused

And
Forgetful about
Our indigenous origins

In
The motherland
Across the Atlantic.

The
Lily white
Master had some

Heat
In his
Pants, hankering for

Serious
Heat in
His bed, generated

With
A female
Slave under his

Orders.
The passion
Was one sided –

All
Over Massa's
Estate, there were

Half-breeds,
Quadroons and
Octoroons who worked

Non-stop –
Ol' Massa's

Occasional matings had

Produced
A whole
Class of slaves

Kept
Ignorant, confused
And forgetful about

Their
African past.
Mass amnesia, it

Seems,
Is intergenerational.
Confusion, a symptom –

People
On the
Street assume that

I
Am something
Other than African.

"Fijian"
Was thrown
At me twice

And
Fiji is
Nowhere near Africa.

"Guatémalan"
Once, "Puerto
Rican," hella times.

Some
People had
Guessed African right.

But
Which nationality?

Ethiopian? Eritrean? Burundi?

Kenyan?
Somali? Sudanese?
Not even close.

Egyptian?
Talk about
A massive stretch.

Right
Continent, wrong
End of it.

The
Mystery disturbs
Me something fierce.

As
History's shown,
The slave trade

Never
Went farther
Than Central Africa –

Although
I was
Born an American

Citizen,
I'm disgusted
To say, my

Nubian
Genes, strong,
Dominant, point a

Straight
Line to
Africa's Western shore.

So
What was

My ancestry then?

Malian?
Senegalese? Liberian?
Or Ivory Coastal?

To
Be precise,
My DNA points

To
A land,
Language and peoples:

Gabon,
Mitsogo and
Tsogo and Ateke.

Ancestors'
Identities reclaimed
Along my tongue.

Gabon,
Mitsogo and
Tsogo and Ateke.

The
Country they
Were abducted from,

The
Language they'd
Spoken before English,

Both
Tribes they'd
Claimed as theirs.

Now
I can
Say with confidence

My
History hadn't

Begun in shackles.

Now
I can
Say with certainty

What
Who my
Ancient forerunners were –

My
Newly found
African past adds

Several
New words
To my vocabulary:

Gabon,
Mitsogo and
Tsogo and Ateke.

Thanks
To you,
Nephew, so determined,

Hungry
For knowledge
Of self, and

Biologists'
Careful research.
For my family

And
For me,
The mystery ends.

---

W: 12.16.17
[ For Mike Allen, Junior. ]

# HOPPIN' JOHN

Another twelve months came and went quickly. Bone-numbing restaurant freezer chill penetrates the house walls. Time to switch on the pivoting electric Lasko© heater. January 1st is here. Fireworks and handguns' explosive sounds combine, bang and boom outside my door. How the rest celebrate, but enough about that. Time to simmer brown rice in vegetable broth, fry slices of Tofurky© Andouille sausage, minced garlic and black-eyed peas in olive oil. In separate pots. Rice, peas, garlic, mock sausage then combined into one pot. Collard greens, oregano, pinch of cayenne pepper, dash of paprika stirred into a spicy winner of a winter-time dinner. Wine glass of sparkling apple cider, candied yams and the steaming dish enjoyed by Black appetites throughout Georgia, Tennessee, Florida and the Carolinas – where it originated – from slavery times to this New Year's Night. Hoppin' John put the heat back into me on a cold, festive evening. Onions are kept out of this dish. Pork sausage definitely stays out.

On this or any
Year, no dead swine shall touch these
Vegan lips of mine.

---

W: 2.27.19
[ For Sue Ellen Pector. ]

# SPOKEN

One stare
Would examine
My movements
And proceed
To follow me
Down well-stocked
Supermarket aisles,
Continuing the stalking,
Expecting theft.

One glance
Would be made
And quickly
Broken looking away
Before taking
Ten paces
Down a moving subway
Train in search of a seat
Away from me,
Hands gripping
Purse a little tighter,
Expecting smash & grab.

One glare
Would pierce my back
Right on contact
Dagger-like
And take
Immediate note
Of my skin tone
After I walk past,
Expecting assault.

*They'd be*
Dreading the unfamiliar,
Xenophobic
Statements
Would be spoken
With just
A look
To tell me

"You're not
Welcome here
Ever"
*If fear had eyes.*

---

W: 4.10.19

# FRAGMENT 2019

I'm not a religious man. Not even a little.

The Bible of Christian love teaches
Hatred and violence,
The very thought of walking into
A church and facing all those sharp-dressed
Hypocrites makes
My stomach do somersaults
And prayers from the heart often
Go unanswered.

Strangely enough,

*What prayer waits on my tongue?*

It won't be a prayer
Wasted on an absentee
Deity. It will, instead,
Be an appeal to fellow
Human beings and here's how I'll release it:

Judge me not
For my looks,
But for my deeds.
The color I have
Is no crime.

---

W: Easter 2019

# DISHONOR

Fresh new swastikas
Spray-painted on Jewish tombstones in France.

Anti-Semitic – *This wound is still tender.*

Black Pentecostal churches
Three set ablaze, skeletal black conditions in Louisiana.

Anti-African – *This wound is still tender.*

Inside two mosques, high-caliber
Bullets flew, devout Muslims lay lifeless in New Zealand.

Islamophobic – *This wound is still tender.*

Seminole maiden
Fictional princess
Wearing Plains Indian
Feathered head-dress,
Moccasins and
Buck-skin dress
Striking Pocahontas pose
For the public and press
Atop rolling float
Mostly paper-maché
Ceremonial queen
For homecoming parades

Sorority girl
Gives sidewalk
Crowds her
Oscar-winning performance

Seminole warrior
Mighty Osceola on horseback
Boldly riding the field
Hands on reins
And battle spear in flames
Eagle feathers attached
His black hair
Under red head-band
Soared in the wind

War paint covers
His scowling face
Opening act for college football games

Frat-house reject
Plays to the bleacher
Crowds with his
Emmy-winning performance –

Florida State has Seminoles
Cleveland has Indians
San Diego State has Aztecs
D.C. has Redskins
Chicago has Blackhawks
Atlanta has Braves

Recycled
Hollywood
Old style
Western

War drums,
War whoops,
War dances,
Tomahawk chop

Made a mockery
Of Native history
Red-face minstrel show –
End the mimicry

Profit, publicity,
Fetishism, dishonor
Go hand in hand
Inside the sports arena.

Anti-Native – *This wound is still tender*

And raw when touched

After 500 years.

W: Ferguson/Nagasaki Anniversary 2019

# CURSIVE WRITER'S CREDO

*Just because you steal something*

Landmass
Continent
Vast territory
The island standing erect
On top of a giant turtle's back

*Doesn't mean you own it!*

Settlement
"Free country"
Colonial territory
"White man's land"
Start of Empire

Gains ill-gotten
With instruments:
Muskets,
Smallpox blankets,
Army swords

*This is still Indian Country*

First ones in the Bay
First villages in the Bay – Yelamu*, Huichin**
First languages used – Ramaytush, Chochenyo
First walkers on this land of oaks
Haven't vanished into the past

*And you live on Ohlone land!*

---

W: 12.11.19
[ For Richard Sanderell, The Cursive Writer. ]

*Yelamu = San Francisco.
** Huichin = Oakland.

# ACCELERATIONISM [ FIRST SALVO ]

They couldn't take
A tactical defeat
In any form.
So just as a gang of bitter
Ex-Confederate soldiers
Straight out of old-school
Spanish/Italian Spaghetti Western
Movies would, another crew of young
Alt-Right fanatics
Try to implement
A laughable ploy:

Another war of secession.

This time, between the races.

Certain eyes took heed to the dispatch
Launched into cyberspace:

"YOU'VE GOT TO DO YOUR PART!
WE'VE GOT TO BRING ON THE COLLAPSE!
NOTHING CAN STOP THE COMING WAR AHEAD!
NOTHING!"

"Nothing"? Really?

The F.B.I.
Federal dragnet
Dragged in
Members of a cadre
Three White heads
Full of delusions
Of bringing pain
In the name
Of ensuring
Caucasian survival.

The "collapse" they desired
Was to come
In hunting people

At the Virginia State Capitol,
Cradle of the old Confederacy,

During a Second Amendment rally.

The rally continued in Richmond as scheduled.

The captured cadre's
Plans for "collapse,"
Multicultural America's
Breakdown in a hurry,
Only bought them

Incarceration, public
Scrutiny and scorn
On television and the internet
As this week's villains. Three White heads
On the media chopping block.

Don't count your D.I.Y. kit guns before they're made.

Before 1500 ammunition rounds could be used,
High-powered assault rifles could be raised,
Magazine clips could be slid on,
Gun rights and police prey could be found,
Or the first salvo of a new Civil War could be shot,

Before the Black Riders, the Brown Berets
Or Antifa crews
Could bust counter-moves,

Accelerationism
Stopped
Accelerating.

W: 2.5.2020

# From the Depths

Unsightly
To look at,
Unbearable
To listen to,
Easy
To avoid
For a moment,

The shamed one
Without clothes

Scales up
Protruding stones
On the encircling wall,
Climbs towards the light above
Away from damp, dark below,
Where she was unjustly held.
In her clenched teeth, a bullwhip.
On her mind, the need to chastise
Humanity for
Casting her
Down there
From notice.

From the depths of an old
Stone well, she comes out
Armed with her leather lash, Truth
Wearing nothing but
Her indignation at
The society she faces,
Invested in defending
All the falseness they so love –

---

W: 2.21.2020
[ Inspired by the painting *Truth Comes
Out of Her Well* by Jean-Léon Gérome. ]

# Disease Breeds Disease

Strange new ailment
Giving pneumonia-like symptoms
Has a ripple effect
Spanning our globe.

Floating on the wind, harm to health,
Diaspora of microbes –
Point of outbreak:
Wuhan, China.

Within a month, fate's transmission
Country by country. Bad news travels fast.
Reported cases of Coronavirus
Breeds a second disease.

One much older, equally contagious,
Easier to spot the signs.
Point of outbreak:
The human mind.

Modes of transmission:
Mainstream media,
Person-to-person contact.
Symptoms include:

Stereotyping,
Side glances,
Spiteful feelings
Disguised as jokes,

Bullying,
Swearing,
Unprovoked assaults,
Avoiding restaurants,

Insulting
Internet memes,
Misinformation,
Discrimination,

Lumping together
Japanese, Korean,

Vietnamese, Laotian
And Thai

Under the heading of
"Chinese,"
International
Travel bans,

Tendency to run from,
Duck and dodge
Straight black
Hair, almond-shaped eyes, yellow skin,

Mistaken
Notion of
"Chinese =
Virus carrier"

And sudden memory loss
Of the simple fact that
Asian lives
Matter, too.

W: 2.23.2020

# One Word

The White man
Uses it to define me
The Black man
Uses it to malign me

One word
Guaranteed to offend me
One word
You feel me? Could tear and rend me!

Raw truth hits home
What do you know?
Knocking wind out of me
Like a body blow!

It afflicted me with shame
Hella dirty and low down
Carrying 400 years of pain
And it's more than a noun

One word
Some fool would call their friend
One word
And it starts with an N

Raw truth hits home
What do you know?
Knocking wind out of me
Like a body blow!

Continued use among Africans
I can't figure
Why they would spit such stupid shit
Rhyming with "bigger"

One word
Taken out of my vocabulary so
One word
Never used on another like me, black as a crow –

W: 2.27.2020

# STICKS AND STONES

TUESDAY FEBRUARY 25TH

NEW DELPHI, INDIA

Today's forecast
Calls for warmer temperatures,
Fair and sunny, with a curiously
Strong chance of precipitation
Taking the forms of

Swinging sticks,
Flying stones
Being thrown
At Muslims.

Don't expect
Prime Minister Modi to help.
He's busy escorting
Two of his illustrious
American guests through
Mahatma Gandhi's retreat, the violent
Reality outside isn't important.

Don't expect
The police to help either.
They're asking detainees
About their religion,
Hand out beatdowns
If they get
The wrong answer,
Force them to sing
The national anthem,
Stand idle, rather pitiless,
At the human storm
Washing over a mosque
With pure animosity and flags

And watching
More sticks swing,
More stones fly,
Fire scorch the city –

The undeclared
War on Islam
Unfolds on the streets
In honor of Lord Ram* –

---

W: 3.1.2020

* Hindu god. Seventh incarnation of Vishnu.

# For Your Survival

FOR YOUR SURVIVAL
NEEDFUL ITEMS TO ACCUMULATE
IN THE WAKE OF A GLOBAL PLAGUE:

N95 face masque
Latex gloves
Rubbing alcohol
Hand soap [ liquid ]
Hand sanitiser
Sanitary wipes
Paper towels [ and plenty ]
Toilet paper [ and plenty ]
Bottled water
Anti-flu medicine
Vitamin C
Lemons
Oranges
Beans
Rice
Pasta
Tomato sauce
Herbal tea [ citrus variety ]
Disinfectants [ like Lysol, Febreze and Clorox ]

And if you're Asian
And living in Southern California,

Handguns and ammunition
For protection
Against unexpected altercations
With people in panic-mode, on that

"Scare thy neighbor" tip,
Afflicted with that other
Disease running rampant:

The one that gives
Sufferers myopia,
Extreme focus on another's
Shade of skin –

*Even oppression*
*Leaves a shadow*
In the time of Corona.

---

W: 3.2020

# THE SHUT DOOR

The shut, locked door
Stands between me
And the disaster
Outside I cannot see

Having no effect
On animals in the least.
It chooses to pounce
On human beasts.

Streets nearly empty,
Cars and buses free to roam.
Shelter from disaster is easy to find
Inside my own home.

Libraries remain closed,
Restaurants will not serve.
Rectangular wood on hinges
Will help me bend the curve

Flattened for a longer, robust life
Beyond respirator masques
And hands covered in latex –
No telling how long this infection lasts.

While the most fool-hardy
Fall to the floor,
Safety is mine, sequestered behind
The shut, locked door.

---

W: 3.2020

# SPIRIT HORSE

Every Spring, as
Trees sprout new leaves,
Aboriginal nation
Reflects and grieves

Long after Justice
Failed them – one more slight –
They remember a beloved sister's
Departure from her family's sight:

At close range, muzzle flash
From a policeman's gun
Panic from a petite Dineh* woman
Dissipated – her life was done.

Street-bound transition
From flesh to spirit
Hoofbeats pound, a steady gallop
And only she could hear it.

Sky-blue eyes, grey spotted body,
Stray horse drew near with a neigh.
Instinctively, she knew
It came to carry her away

From a White man's world that shown her
Nothing but disrespect –
She climbed onto the steed's bare back,
Wrapped her arms around its massive neck

And finally rode off
On a distant course

To her peaceful, eternal repose
On the Spirit Horse.

---

W: 3.28.2020
[ For Loreal Tsingine – 1989 – 2016. ]

* What the Navajo Indians call themselves.

# LONE WOLF

Long before
This perilous time,
Long before
This unhealthy clime,

Long before
Death tolls in every land,
Long before
Infection held the upper hand,

I've distanced myself from the crowd –
Strong intention from my heart –
To extract myself from willful
Ignorance which I had no part,

To secede from the arrogant,
Their every petty construction,
To leave before they overwhelm me –
Orgies of reputation destruction.

I have more respect for animals
Than for the human race.
Six feet apart, for me,
Isn't enough space.

I've met some good people –
They're few and far between –
Because my heart felt wounded countless times,
I shun the social scene.

These are words of experience
From one humble creature.

I roam the harsh wilderness
A lone wolf – by nature.

W: 4.4.2020

# BARREN

Barren

Streets – Oakland's 74 miles closed
To cars – Mayor Schaaf prioritizes
Two-wheeled exercise and safety
For gentrifiers.

Barren

Subway stations – Social
Distancing maintained
To the extreme. Underground
Solid concrete ghost town.

Barren

Hotel rooms – They'd make better
Shelter in place for the homeless than being
Warehoused in close quarters on mats. Existing method:
Good way to get infected.

Barren

Shelves – Inside the supermarket –
The spirit of hoarding
Cleared them of supplies.
Long line of humanity outside are in for a nasty surprise.

Barren

Heart – There's
Nothing left dwelling in the husk for some.
Nothing left but hostility – Blame for sickness
Lands on descendants of Asia.

Barren

Describes this reality, re-configured
By rapid infection – Humanity homebound –
There's no reverting back

To normal after this.

I survived
Ten presidents, the residual terror of four
Foreign wars, power outages, outbursts of nature,
A petrol shortage, evictions and homelessness.

I will survive this, even as this contaminated air
World quickly goes

Barren.

---

W: 4.21.2020

# Masques Up

There was a time
When wearing a masque
In public was equated w/ anti-system
Protests in the streets, attending the
Most extravagant, fun balloon
& paper streamer-strewn
Costume ball @ best
& crime at worst –

It's the Law now
To throw the masques up.
Simple, repurposed
Cloth covering our faces, concealing all
But our eyes. Looking fresh

From a steam train
Robbery Old West style
Or a Black Bloc
Putting some smash on the blue block
That redlines & forecloses
& holds money simultaneously
Chase Bank© –

To throw the masques up
Is an exercise of
Good judgment now. Invasion of our persons
Held back w/ a new school
Protection spell. Just add cloth
Firmly over nose & mouth.
Continued being assured against

Robbery of our lives
By a thief so intrusive,
Another murderer unseen –
Only far more elusive.

W: 5.4.2020

# Moving Game

On a hunting trip,
Father and son
Brought their rifles –
And a Magnum

Rolled in a white pick-up truck
Through a quiet, tree-lined domain
Driven closer on the heels
Of moving game

Cornered on the roadside –
Hunters stepped forward to attack.
Hot lead poured into their prey.
His skin was Black.

Running athlete – "Suspected burglar"
The line they told the cops later.
What would you expect
From Georgia backwoods haters?

The New South
Façade disrupted with a passion,
The Old South
Returned in homicidal fashion.

Now the hunters are captured and caged
And rightfully accused.
Father and son find themselves fair game
For the rage that rage produced.

W: 5.11.2020
[ For Ahmaud Arbery – 1996 – 2020. ]

# THE FALLEN

[ Song lyrics ]

Now is the day
To find a way
To loosen pain and mourn

One hundred thousand
Women and men
From this existence, they're torn

Say a eulogy
Amidst this tragedy
Visited on the now-deceased

One hundred thousand
Women and men
Fallen from a new/cruel disease

CHORUS: Let's sing this requiem
        Never forget the fallen
        Let's sing this requiem
        Never forget the viral victims

        While the heart aches

Light a candle
Speak your preamble
To remembrances of old friends

One hundred thousand
Women and men
Together, they met tragic ends

Contagion never stops
We've fallen like raindrops
From an angry grey sky above

One hundred thousand
Women and men
This disease won't stop us from showing love

[ Repeat chorus ]

REFRAIN: Acknowledge them all [ 6 times ]

        While the heart aches

W: Marilyn Monroe Birthday 2020

# CONTAINMENT

Leave it to the system
To place a harsh limit
On Black bodies'
Freedom of movement

At sundown,
Social life ends
At nightfall,
For yourself and your friends.

Leave it to the system
To manage to avail
Making Black homes
Seem more like jail,

Somewhere to report to
When the sun slowly sinks
In the western horizon –
This goes against instincts –

Leave it to the system
To push a harsh limit
On Black activity –
Selective enforcement –

The night is meant
To be enjoyed by everyone,
To dance and dine,
To party and have fun.

Isolation works well in
Keeping away Coronavirus.
"Indoors at 8"

Only inspires us

To defy mass containment –
Motherfuck you
And your stop and frisk
And your racist curfew!

W: 6.6.2020

# PROPER BURIAL

Death begets
More death.

The killing of real
Innocent Black people begets
The removal of old
Caricatures of Black people.

Aunt Jemima
Greets us with a smile
From a pancake batter box
And a pancake syrup bottle over breakfast.

Old girl gets around.

Uncle Ben
Greets us with a smile
From a box of dry
Instant white rice in preparation of dinner.

Dude's so happy to be servile.

The killing of real
Innocent Black people
On America's mean streets begets
The removal of old
Racist cartoons,
Exaggerations of Black people
Who should've died decades ago.

The coffins are waiting

For Auntie and Uncle.
Stick them in. Heap dirt on them.
Mounds of dirt. And hope to fuck
No one exhumes their plots.

Jemima and Ben,
Those stereotypical
Visitors to our meals,

More than deserve final
Commencement from our view,
A proper burial.

Ring the bell.
Alert the neighbors.
And the White folks, too.

DING! DONG!
THE MASCOTS ARE DEAD!

---

W: 6.18.2020

# PICCOLO ORSO*

The front window-sills of houses
In Noe Valley,
San Francisco's
High-end suburb on the hill
Above the Mission,
Are galleries for
Placards these days.

Held fast to pane glass with Scotch Tape©
Are tack-board admonishments
To neighbors unnerved by
The continued march of Corona,
Bearing words that soothe:

EVERYTHING WILL BE OK.
WE WILL SURVIVE.
WE WILL GET THROUGH THIS.

And then, Mister
Teddy Bear makes his appearance.

Stuffed wool, thread and varnished button eyes
Comprises our friend's being.
Little Teddy sits
In the window-sill of a house
Soaking up the morning sun,
Just chilling, passing small
Children on Jersey Street
Enjoy his cute, adorable,
Calming presence. Tiny fingers point up to their find:

Little Teddy
Kicking it, calm and lounging
Next to a hand-drawn
Placard, reminding block residents
What Hunter's Point, Sunnydale,
Seminary, Eastmont and I
Have always known to be fact:

BLACK LIVES MATTER.

A child's bed-time companion
Moved on up
To the front of the house.
He's on constant display
Like a hard plastic preening
Mannequin in Neiman Marcus©'
Store-front window,

There in the window-sill
As a plush symbol
For these strange days,
When breathing the air
Without a masque on
Around others
Is unhealthy.

Little Teddy
Reassures us
That these days
Don't have to be scary.
He tells us

Non-verbally
That if we stay safe,
If we keep our connections
Despite the isolation,
Despite the miles,

EVERYTHING WILL BE OK.

---

W: Summer Solstice 2020

* ITALIAN: "Little bear."

# FEAR OF ASSAULT

*During the COVID-19 global pandemic...*

I fear sudden weakness
I fear an assault
Worse than a hate crime,
Worse than the occult

By some assailant
Much smaller than me
Since this disaster began,
Insecurity –

It could travel through nostrils,
Pass my wet tongue,
Plummet down the trachea
And flood my lungs

With so much phlegm,
This brother couldn't breathe,
Hacking with persistent cough –
No goddamn reprieve

Body burning like an open flame
Scalding my head –
The systemic immunity
Breakdown I dread –

This infection is real

I'm feeling its impact
Earth brings out her dead
Majority Native and Black

Filling hospitals and freezer trucks
Caused by bacteriological hex
Somewhere down the line
I might become next

To be one with the darkness
Against my mortal will

I've no wish to find out
If a mystery can kill

And it has
Made early graves and much more
Some other sensation
Stirs within my core

Call it resilience –
You probably felt it, too –
These days, I'm a busy man.
I've got too much living to do.

---

W: Canadian Aboriginal Day 2020
[ For Jennifer A. Minotti. ]

# Oathsworn

For a mere
Three seconds
On camera,
Filmed in austere
Black and white,
You'd given the statement
Which caught me off-guard,
Spoken the words
I never heard
Any celebrity say:

*I stand against hate.*

That oath you'd made
For this little P.S.A.
Had the usual Hollywood
Polish and pretence
Missing from it.

It didn't smack
Of someone gunning
For an Emmy nomination.
It didn't smack
Of someone reading
Phrases from a teleprompter
Like a vapid TV news reporter.
It didn't smack
Of someone auditioning
For some unspecified role.

Although you received far less
Screen-time than
"The A-list" types,
You sounded committed
To use your privilege to aid
A struggle without end
Where I'm the target.
The other big names and faces
Sounded more willing to save
Careers from ruin than showing up

Against organized violence.

Police terror is racial terror –

Given those circumstances,
I'm inclined to believe
A fitness personality
Over Pop singers and movie stars.

The advert you appeared in
Had proven to
Hinder more than help,
More performative than conducive
To a cause centuries-old,
A libratory cause
Larger than us both –

You've taken an oath.
On camera.
So what happens next?

Would you stand
With my people
When White Supremacy
Moves in close
For the kill?

Would you stand
With families
As their loved ones
Transform into
Hashtags?

Would you rush
To my side
If acid tongues
Seared my honor,
Insulted my color?

Would you fight
With the same
Conviction as you did
With fellow gymnasts, army of survivors, backing
A lecherous monster in doctor's guise into a corner?
I'm not asking

To be saved.
I'm asking if I could count
On your support of
My besieged people.

Since the ancient
Southern slave revolts,
Africans were at the forefront
Resisting genocide,
Resisting criminalization,
Our status as hated.

But it doesn't
Hurt to have
A reliable ally
On one's side.

And that lady
On the Silk©
Organic soy milk
Unsweet carton

Might be a good one.

---

W: 6.26.2020
[ For Aly Raisman. ]

# OUT FRONT

*I am grateful for…*

The arched roof above my head
The twin rafters with
The twin lights, holding it in place
The four walls surrounding me
The two windows with
The two Venetian blinds, down & shut at all times
The red brick floor below my feet
The wooden shelves full of books & movies
The VHS by themselves & DVDs in clear totes
The Keetsa© mattress I sleep on
The melatonin that helps me sleep
The vegan food in my fridge, a meat-free zone
The fruit & vegetable juices I savor
The filtered water I drink more than tap shit
The hardcover journal notebooks and
The rollerpoint pens I use to express myself
The shower I use, even though I'm a bathtub man
The Hewlett Packard laptop computer aiding creation of
The once and future poetry volumes
The Samsung© TV & VCR/DVD player combo
The little house in East Oakland I call home
The vast collection of political slogan t-shirts
I wear the convictions of my heart
On my chest
SOMETIMES ANTI-SOCIAL ALWAYS ANTI-RACIST
Remains a personal favorite but
BEING BLACK IS NOT A CRIME
Gets me the most love on the street

But most of all

*I am grateful for…*

The bus drivers
The firefighters
The restaurant
Delivery drivers
The subway train conductors

The launderette clerks
The grocery store workers

The farmer's market workers
Which I happen to be one
The doctors
The nurses
The paramedics
The pharmacy workers
The protestors for the rights of all Black lives
The dead and the living
The mutual aid collectives
Giving food, water, medicine and household
Items to the people living hand to mouth
During this goddamn pandemic
And long before

All the heroes
Out front
In our service
Seeing to our immediate
Survival needs

They could use the praise

And you don't need
Super powers
To be a hero

Just be there
Out front
For us –

W: Stonewall Anniversary 2020
[ For Jennifer A. Minotti. ]

# Four Spirits

They ascended to the clouds
From an explosion site –
Four spirits, six doves.

Rubble made from a chapel
Sixteenth Street Baptist –
Four spirits, six doves.

Klansman's dynamite
Burst and produced –
Four spirits, six doves.

Policeman's and teenager's
Ire gunned down two boys –
Four spirits, six doves.

Four little girls
Perpetual youth –
Four spirits, six doves.

Forever in preparation
For Sunday school –
Four spirits, six doves.

The first sits on a bench,
The second stands and waits –
Four spirits, six doves.

The third ties a bow on
The fourth girl's dress –
Four spirits, six doves.

The fourth girl frees white birds
From the captivity of her hands –
Four spirits, six doves.

These birds had names in previous lives:
Denise, Carol, Cynthia, Addie Mae, Virgil, Johnny –
Four spirits, six doves.

W: 7.9.2020
[ Inspired by a sculpture by Elizabeth MacQueen. ]

# SAMARITAN

Anyone else
Would've left that Far Right
Reactionary sprawled on the concrete
To bleed out, suffer in his
Paroxysms of serious hurt, receive
Disaster of the steel-toed kind.

But not you.

The Good Samaritan
Reflex kicked in,
Wouldn't let you
Abandon someone in need of help.

Distinctions such as
"Friend" and "foe" didn't matter.
Whom you saw laying at your feet
Wasn't an "enemy.'

Just an injured man.

So you lifted him in your arms,
Slung him over your shoulder
Like a heavy sack of laundry,
Carried him in a firefighter's hold
With a cordon of protection around you,
Your four comrades having your back,
Moving past a raging crowd
And riot-cops

With the boisterous sounds
Of the inner-city battleground
In both of your ears –
Football songs, national anthem,
Protest chants, flares and smoke grenades –

Maybe you thought

One dead
White man
Wasn't going to bring back

One dead
Black man
In Minneapolis,

One dead
Black woman
In Louisville,

One dead
Black man
In a Wendy's© parking lot in Atlanta,

Martyrs from American
Racial flashpoints –

Maybe you thought

That injured man's
Life was more worthy of salvation
Than stone monuments to previous wars,
Winston Churchill's statue
And the Cenotaph.

Descriptions such as
"Hero" didn't matter either.
You're just a man protecting
A neck that wasn't your own

And you wanted
Equality, right that minute,
For your children,
For your grandchildren,
For the generations ahead,
For England and troubled America,
If we can get past
Misunderstanding and factions. Brother,

I wish I had
Your Good Samaritan
Resolve.

---

W: 7.13.2020
[ For Patrick Hutchinson. ]
[ Inspired by a photograph by Dylan Martinez from the
international news service Reuters. ]

# WHINE

One of the most annoying things
I've heard of late
Was caught one morning whilst riding
A B.A.R.T. subway train from Oakland to S.F.

Some lady in sunglasses boarded
And took a seat eight paces from mine,
Complained to her friend on a Smartphone
About how she couldn't wait for

Everything to be restored
Back to normal.

What was considered
Normal
Before the Pandemic

Did damage
To certain
Races, classes, sexes, sexualities,
Abilities and nationalities

Of people, species
Of animals and this
Nurturing old Earth
Herself.

I don't want a
Return to the old ways,
To methods of mayhem. I want to see change
For the better, after this global sickness subsides.

So you want things
Back to normal, huh?
Got any cheese and crackers
To go with that whine?

W: 7.16.2020

# BROKEN CONTRACT

There's one high, steep mountain
We, the ambitious, must climb
To reach our sweetest dreams

And after numerous
Attempts at advancing
Up that same
Monolithic rock, almost touching the moon,

The White elite above
Still can't stand to see
Any brother, any sister
On the come up –

A level playing field
Is a threat to them.
Economic freedom
Is a threat to them.

*The closer we get to the summit,*
The farther down
We fall from
Being pushed by
The few nearest
To the top.

It's when the earthen floor
Surrounding the mountain
Fills with fallen, fractured
Bodies, dark of skin

That shows
The social contract between
White America and Black America
Being broken.

---

W: 7.23.2020
[ For Trevor Noah and Kimberly Jones. ]

# SLAVESTATE

The South's
Original sin
Hadn't missed
The North.

Dutch and English
Settlers in colonial times
Bought and worked
By the head imported

Living commodities
Subjects of kidnapping
From Africa, South Carolina,
Forced to build the material wealth

At the ironworks,
Farms, apple orchards,
For a more
Condescending kind.

Social codes,
Bullwhip brutality
Black and Native together
In abject captivity –

The nasty
Little secret
The Garden State
Continues to omit from their ongoing story –

It will take
More than an apology
From a politician's mouth
For us to develop any trust in systems, Northern or Southern –

W: 7.24.2020
[ For Bruce Hansen – 1947 – 2019. ]

# Bold-Faced Lie

Accused of a vicious crime
Four Black men
World War 2 veterans
Two of them
Captured by Sheriff
Willis McCall
Confined in Lake County Jail
One by one
Handcuffed to a lead
Pipe on the basement ceiling, shirtless,
Beaten with blackjacks
Broken soda bottle glass on bare feet
What the deps called
"Securing confessions"
Suspects bore marks
From the violent process –
Sheriff's smooth talk
Couldn't hold back entirely
Enormous ring of white
Hoods and robes enclosed
At the front of the jail –
K.K.K. super-klavern all
Crunk from bloodlust
Crann Tara ruled that moment
Night Of The Fiery Crosses
Houses nearby burnt to the ground
Black exodus, fright and flight
Arson and abhorrence
In the land of orange groves
One of the four accused
Took flight on his own
Through the woods, his biggest mistake:
Resting under a tree

The posse's shotguns boomed his way
And the four became three –

Trial in session
Judge Truman Futch presided
The three deemed guilty

Before the verdict was in
Before an all-White jury

Convictions:
Death penalty for two
Life sentence for one
Demoralizing state of affairs –
Lynching in the courtroom – Possible
Second trial taken to a much higher place:
U.S. Supreme Court
Thurgood Marshall for the defense
Convictions overturned
The fruit borne from an appeal –
Sheriff stops car at roadside at night
While transporting his two prisoners
From Raiford State Penitentiary
An order to change a faulty tire
Turned into shooting
Execution style, six shots flew

Thirty-eight Special in McCall's hand
And the three became two –

One behind bars and aging,
One wounded yet threatened
With the electric chair –
Re-trial in Marion County
Thurgood Marshall, future
De-segregation hero,
Back on the case –

Re-trial
Rerun
Of the first
And worst

Until the hand
Of Governor Collins
Reduced sentence
From death to life
For Walter Irvin,
The last Groveland Boy.

And all that

Needless drama began

With a skinny Southern

White country girl
With an abusive husband

Wandering solo into the lonely concrete block
Bartoft's Café.
She told the young man who
Invited her inside one story

And told Sheriff McCall a totally
Different one, of night-time
Violation in a parked car.
A bold-faced lie
Of rape.

---

W: 7.27.2020

# GOLDEN NECTAR

Opening the refrigerator door,
I reached out for
The plastic bottle of liquid
Golden euphoria I needed.

The true
Pause that refreshes,
Pure as sunlight,
Ice-cold sunshine,
Adds life
To taste-buds, always
The really
Real thing,
Have it
And enjoy,
Taste the feeling

You won't get
From the fizzy
Caffeinated brown stuff
From a shiny red
Aluminum can with
A white wave. No euphoria there.

It's

Sweeter
Than a kiss
From the woman
You most desire,
Enjoyable
Like a moist
Tongue fencing another moist
Tongue inserted inside your mouth,
Better for the heart
Than a romantic
Fling does
In the very beginning –

Only a fruit grown

In the Philippines,
Brown and prickly

On the outside,
Soft and sun-yellow
On the inside,
Could elicit such sensations – Golden

Satisfaction
Poured
From bottle
To glass
To straight
Down my gullet –

Opening the refrigerator door,
I reached out for
The plastic bottle of pleasing
Golden nectar I needed.

Chilled pineapple juice from the shelf.

---

W: 8.3.2020

# Not the Time

[ Song lyrics ]

Now is not the time
To be silent
Now is not the time
To turn your eyes from the violent

Now is not the time
To show your poker face
Now is not the time
To walk from attacks on another race

CHORUS: Not the time [ 3 TIMES ]
            To ignore another's distress
            Not the time [ 3 TIMES ]
            To side with those who oppress

            Not the time

Now is not the time
To be silent
Now is not the time
To turn your head from the violent

Now is not the time
To hold on to a selfish choice [ of comfort ]
When you see oppression,
Remove your fear and raise your voice

[ REPEAT CHORUS ]

Not the time
To give the cold shoulder
This is the time
For this hate to be over [ TWICE ]

W: 8.12.2020

# In Three Stanzas

for Andrea Blackman and Rashad Rayford

*I, too, am America, but...*

The exclusion
From tomorrow,
The dinner table
Admits privileged company still,
My color continues
To be a strike against me,
Despite the claims of equality,
The back door
Is still the only entry point
And the dinner guests
See me more
As far less
Than they –

*Today, Justice is...*

Holding an intense conversation with me
At home about the crimes this country
Had committed in her midst. She ain't blind.
This Native American sister with braids
Is going deep into the well of her people's
History, how they were suddenly made
Prisoners and underdogs on their own
Land, a large mass of dispossessed.
Let me tell you, Justice wasn't all about
Sorrow. She laid some hope on me, for
Justice is proposing on how all the iniquities
Of the past can be reversed. The best,
Smartest ally this darker brother can have –

*I will write the power by...*

Becoming the hero
I need to be
For myself
And for my long
Suffering race.

Speak out
When the blustery
Voice of hate

Tries to assert itself
Over mine.
To silence
This verbal drama
That divides us,
Creates the wrong
Social distancing.
That's what
The powers that be
Count on –
They shall have
No excuse from my end –

W: 9.8.2020

# Duck Hill

THE DEGREE OF CIVILISATION IN A SOCIETY
CAN BE JUDGED BY ENTERING
ITS PRISONS.

Fyodor Dostoevsky
Russian writer
Hit the figurative
Nail on its head
When he commenced
Those words to paper –

Montgomery County, Mississippi, 1937:

Bootjack McDaniels
Red Townes
Witnessed justice,
Like money,
Changing hands

From courtroom justice
Before a black-robed magistrate
To Southern justice
Before a howling mob
Wanting to stain their white hands red.

Bootjack McDaniels
Red Townes
Were pulled deep
Into the maniacal heart
Of a tormentors' circle overgrown

A few bad men
Overpowered Winona
Town Sheriff's deputies to grab those two
Quickly, orderly,
But far from quietly.

Bootjack McDaniels
Red Townes
Took an unsettling school-bus ride
While hog-tied
And terrified

School-bus, cars, trucks, midday
Country motorcade rolled
One mile from the grocery store
Where this all began – Five hundred
Gathered in the woods of Duck Hill to see

Bootjack McDaniels
Red Townes
Shirtless, tied to trees
With rope and steel chains
Unwilling stars in a show provided for the deranged.

Confession extraction technique:
Plumber's blowtorch
Bare backs blackened further,
Exposed flesh sizzled from
The touch of hot flame.

Bootjack McDaniels
Scorched, then shot.
Red Townes
Burnt alive.
Strapped down, charred

Husks of men.
Dual warnings to other

Black men to never
Raise a shotgun against a White man.
A shopkeeper, least of all.

Given such a shred of history,
Such demonstrations of cruelty,
Delusions of supremacy,
I can do
Dostoevsky one better:

THE DEGREE OF CIVILISATION IN A SOCIETY
CAN BE JUDGED BY THE WAY IT TREATS
PEOPLE OF AFRICAN DESCENT.

W: 10.2.2020

# Bro Way

Splotch of Krylon© black
Paint changed the name
And character of downtown
Oakland's main drag

From Broadway
To Bro Way and it shows.

When the businesses closed down
Behind thick plywood and nails,
Polychromatic murals went up,
Coating them with words and images.
Open air, free of charge
Art exhibit over two miles wide.

Aerosol can-made homages
To the non-Caucasians no longer here –
Bayard Rustin, Ray Charles, John Lewis, Sandra Bland,
Emmett Till, George Floyd, Breonna Taylor –
And heroes still
Among the living –
Angela Davis, Cornel West, Boots Riley, Stevie Wonder –

Different sceneries in different hues declare
Liberation for the Africans here in the West.
The dead deserve justice,
The living, respect –

Who would've thought civil unrest,
Shattered glass, protestors battling cops,

Could bring a great surfeit
Of beautiful paint, art for blocks?

W: Indigenous Peoples Day 2020

# UNDICI [ MARZO 1891 ]*

Venomous slur from a dying man's parted lips
Someone to blame his shooting on – the Captain** knew that score
New Orleans police announced total war
On the Sicilians, who first arrived there in ships
And the entire Crescent City flips
Over that and Blacks shopping at every migrant's store
Arrest, trial, acquit, mistrial – Locals were sore
Nooses and weapons in the mob's fingertips
Orleans Parrish Prison – mighty stone fort –
Had its door battered open, the bum-rush immense
Hide and seek with a malicious consequence
In the prison yard and cellblock, rifles fired then
Caught nine, two hung outside – a ghastly sport
Final offering to a vilifying press: Eleven lynched Italian men.

---

W: 10.14.2020

* ITALIAN: "Eleven [ March 1891 ]."
** William O'Connor, captain of the New Orleans
   Police Department, who found Police Chief
   David Hennessey mortally wounded on the
   night of October 15, 1890.

# NOTHING TO CELEBRATE

Italian blood mixes
With West African
And a minuscule
Amount of true
American in these veins.
The blood of three
Cultures I do
Not fit into
Blend inside this body.

Never, in five decades,
Have I looked up to
This explorer I was
Told to revere back in elementary school.
This Italian explorer
Teachers gave lessons about

Who discovered nothing.
Upon taking a long
Sail from a Spanish harbor,
His ship had gotten lost at sea
And eventually made landfall
Someplace in the Caribbean.
There was a full culture in place
And native inhabitants –
Taíno, they called themselves –
The explorer thought would be perfect

For life-long enslavement in Europe.
And those were the ones who
Didn't meet with his crewman's swords.

The shame of America
Had shown its gruesome face
At Orleans Parish Prison,
Afternoon, March 14, 1891. Thousands in a mob.
It was "Pick Your Prey Day." Sicilians were chosen.
Nine perished from gunshots, inside the jail.
Two were strung up, outside from lamp-posts.

The lynchings of eleven Southern Italians,
Apparent evil, as lynchings of any

Number of Blacks, highly praised in papers
South and North, must've chewed away at
President Benjamin Harrison's conscience,
Moved the man to do two things:

Pay $25,000 restitution
To the victims' families and
Create a holiday so Italians
Are stitched into the colorful American fabric.

Out of a long list of famous
Italian names,
The explorer
So-called was selected.
Leonardo DaVinci Day
Would've been interesting on calendars.

Natives feel relief,
Most Italians feel rage
During this age
Of historical markers
Coming down from public places.
Engraved offences
Removed from our faces.

No hero of mine
Would enslave the Taíno, the Arawak
Or any indigenous people,
Ship them to Europe
As potential property,
Order his crew
To carve off
Hands and noses
If he wasn't given
Cotton and gold payments.
No, any hero of mine
Wouldn't be an inventor
Of the old protection racket
And a straight-up
Torturer and killer –

The heroes
I have chosen

Liberated,
Not exterminated –

The heroes
I have chosen
Had triumphed over evil,
Out of love for their people –

A holiday
For Nat Turner
Have yet to make datebooks.
A statue
For Tecumseh
Have yet to sculpted and erected.

Second Monday
Every October
Is wasted
On a bloodthirsty fuck
Who never
Saw America.

Nothing to celebrate.

Here lies
Chirstopher Columbus
Despised icon
On the town square floor,
Finally brought down.
The fury of millions
Pulled hard on the ropes –

W: 11.20.2020

# PRECIPICE

Gladly say goodbye
To the proven nightmare,
These past
Four years –

The precipice
On which I stand
Is crowded with
The eager

Waiting on
Cures for
Both viruses.
The one
Ailing bodies,
The one
Extinguishing love.

Smooth transition
Into another era,
Focus of everybody's
Endogenic wishes, appealing even to my jaded self.

*When I close my eyes,*
*I hear the popular song of*

"What Now?"

___

W: 11.23.2020

# Rolling Out

"DUE TO THE ELECTION
VICTORY OF OPPONENT
JOE BIDEN, OUR PRESIDENT'S
STAND-BY ORDER HAS BEEN RESCINDED.

WE'RE ROLLING OUT."

Rolling out
To save Western Civilization –
They love to blow
On that dog whistle

Rolling out
To prevent White genocide –
They obviously
Don't read statistics

Rolling out
For the Whites who built Western society alone –
They obviously
Forsaken the slaves who raised up wood, mortar & stone

Rolling out
To give multi-cultural populace
Their own racial reckoning
For the loss of a "fearless leader"

Rolling out
To keep America great –
On the streets like no other –
Maybe Hitler's Brownshirts* and Nazi skinhead gangs

Rolling out
With American flags in their horde –
Proud to sow intimidation, reap domestic terror
Quasi-military boys so proud to be so damn wrong –

---

W: Thankstaking 2020

* *Das Sturmabteilung* [ SA – "Storm Unit" ].

# FIVE WORD CHALLENGE

This year 2020
Left us *rushing*
Toward apocalypse
With multiple causes
Unseen *vaporizer* of billions
Without warning
Coronavirus leading the charge –
Humanity travelling on *slalom* course of ice
To the end most disbelieved

Some wildfires here,
Some super storms there,
Tail end of tyrannical
American rule right in the middle –

Gone is the *schadenfreude**
Spewing from orange face,
Repeated by loyal
Flag-waving, red cap bigot followers

And here's to hoping

Gone will be our increasing isolation,
Our lockdown *situation* –
Vaccines are appearing, pharmaceutical lab
Works-in-progress –
I'll trust one
When the new vice president
Herself takes a needle shot –

---

W: 12.14.2020
[ For Paul Casey. ]

* German: "Harm joy." Pleasure gained from another's
trouble.

# Anti-Social Network

Listen, sheltered one:
The Black body poses no threat to you.
He's offering lawn-cutting services
Or just passing through

The suburban neighborhood deemed safe –
Dream of a city dweller –
Maybe you locked up your
Sense of fairness in the cellar.

Would you be so quick
To reach for your cellphone,
Type in complaints, take pics
Of every Black man that roamed?

Station houses are flooded with
Aspersions, thanks to you.
False crime reports
Help the police state continue.

Neighborhood watch gone digital,
Armed with audacity to profile.
Anti-social network Nextdoor
Runs on speech – racist & vile.

W: 12.24.2020

# BESTIA INTERNA*

an open letter to racist bullies

The stiff
Index finger
Singled me out from many
The nickname
You gave me
One step from seeing harm
Nettlesome
Shouting match
What you start shall be finished
No reason
For this strife but your

Strong dislike of my skin complexion –

*The air between you and me*

Is concrete thick
With our tension.

Anyone taking delight
In inflicting pain
On another without
Game-plan or good rationale
Is nothing

Short of being a monster.

Well, guess what?

*There's a monster inside me, too.*

Fact.

Guess what else?

It wants the blood
Of a hater on its claws.

Your every word,

Your every act,
Your hand you wish
To shove me with

Breaks the lock
On the cage within,
Encouraging my snarling
Inner beast to run out.

Better pray to whatever
God you believe in
That the monster in me
Doesn't lunge for the throat
Of the sniveling
Coward in you.

---

W: 1.13.

*Latin & Italian: "Inner beast."

# IOLA

for Michelle Duster, great-granddaughter of Ida B. Wells-Barnett.

Pages of the *Living Way*
Newspaper, which reached readers
Every week, was how the public
Saw eloquent words and met

Her, Iola

Told many of her harrowing tale
Of injustice turned resistance:
Boarded a steam train for work, Nashville bound,
First class seat taken, comfy ride for

Her, Iola

The White conductor disapproved,
Did his damnedest to remove
Consign to a smoky, crowded
"Colored only" car, disregard for

Her, Iola

Promptly answered him with her teeth,
Fastened onto pale hand, bitten deep,
White passengers cheered as she was dragged out –
This episode wasn't over for

Her, Iola

Contested the egregious matter in court
Chesapeake & Ohio Railroad, her opponents
The judge awarded $500 in damages
Soon to be lost, company appeal against

Her, Iola

It was the sudden shooting of three
Successful Black grocers, all good friends, because
Southern White businessmen despised competition,
That brought this schoolteacher to her typewriter, motivation for

Her, Iola

Shone truth's light on ghastly wrongs
Between the *Evening Star & Free Speech*
Until hatred's fire was set to her printing press
Added stress on the journalistic princess, Memphis off-limits to

Her, Iola

New York City, Northern refuge
Safe enough to continue the deluge:
Reports on Southern horrors acquired
From talks with victims' relations, fleshed out by

Her, Iola

The record of the South continued to go red
From any hick town producing Nubian dead
From shotgun shells, bullets, fire and rope
Enclosed around necks of humanity, counted by

Her, Iola

That never failed to chill the soul
Commonly used method of control
When Blacks came up, supremacy cut them down –
Allegations of rape of White women found false by

Her, Iola

Chicago, England, Wales, Scotland – wherever she did a speech
On the crime of lynching – Preach, lady, preach –
America isn't the land of the free
If you're not free to be Black, the gist from

Her, Iola

"Separate but equal" – official falsehood
Separate and sub-standard facilities – never good
Signs at public places turned away dark faces –
The basis for a fight for equality, which began with

Her, Iola.

W: Mardi Gras 2021

# PRETTY

Pretty
Comes
In
All shades.

Vanilla ice cream,
Creamed coffee,
Creamy peanut butter,
Caramel,
Honey,
Cinnamon,
Pecan,
Milk chocolate,
Dark chocolate,
Molasses.

Delicious hues,
Sweet hues,
Tempting and
Watering mouths.

I could never
Understand why racism
Continues to exist
With multi-culturalism in the midst.
Careful, conscious societal maneuvers
From prejudice to justice.
But I understand
Far less colorism,
That sickening division
Among members of the same race
Along the lines of complexion.

Who has melanin?
How much melanin?
And who looks beautiful?

The division is large
And super-charged
Among females

Still performing

Plastic comb tests
Checking for kinks in hair,
Still performing
Brown paper bag tests
In their minds.

"Light girls are stuck up."
"Dark girls are envious and mean."

Divisive notions
Grown out of polluted soil,
Near-European grade:

"In absence of whiteness,
Go for brightness.
You'll get the goods with lightness,
For lightness is right-ness."

Who decides

Who is pretty enough?
Who is Black enough?
What verdict does the bedroom mirror
Give the longer one stares into it?

Sisters lashing out
At each other,
Not once knowing
They're all royalty.

Brothers ignore
Some sisters,
Not once knowing
The queens they're missing out on –

Nature has a way
Of passing out
In equal shares

Beauty, brought to the surface
As distinct physical traits, female to female

Hair, eyes, noses, lips, skin –

Apparently, nature likes variety

As I do.

What catches my eye,
Appeals to my eye.

Pretty comes in all shades of black.

---

W: 3.11.21
[ Inspired by the autobiographical essay *A Colorist In Recovery* by Stephanie J. Gates and the documentary *Light Girls.* ]

# Print Appearances

Doctrine > Synchronized Chaos [ Webzine ]: April 28, 2009 and The Red Pill [ 'Zine ]: December 31, 2010.

Blood And Soil > Bay Area Generations #54 [ Souvenir Event Chapbook ]: February 26, 2018.

Concrete Altar > Bay Area Generations #61: September 24, 2018, Leaves Of Ink [ Website ]: October 18, 2018 and Tuck Magazine [ Webzine ]: October 19, 2018.

Unholy Beast > Decolonewz #12 [ Newspaper ]: Fall 2018.

Shorn > Leaves Of Ink: November 4, 2018 and Dimestore Review [ Webzine ]: January 31, 2019.

Without Teeth > Civil Liberties United [ Anthology ]: Pease Press, 2019.

Rusty Gallows > Leaves Of Ink: September 30, 2018 and Shrew #13 [ Webzine ]: February 2020.

Hoppin' John > The Raven's Perch [ Webzine ]: August 11, 2020.

Dishonor > 2019-20 San Diego Poetry Annual [ Anthology ]: San Diego Entertainment and Arts Guild/Garden Oak Press, 2020.

Cursive Writer's Credo > Flashes of Brilliance [ Website ]: July 19, 2020.

From The Depths > The Raven's Perch: August 11, 2020.

Disease Breeds Disease > The Voices Project [ Website ]: April 13, 2020, We Carry Us: An N.Y.S.A.I. Press Project – New York Public Library Saint George Centre [ Facebook Page ]: April 11, 2020 and The Po' People's Survival Guide Thru Covid-19 and The Virus of Poverty [ Anthology ]: Poor Press, 2020.

For Your Survival > Dyst #2 [ Magazine ]: June 2020 [ Edited ].

The Shut Door > The Po' People's Survival Guide Thru Covid-19 and The Virus of Poverty: Poor Press, 2020 and Dyst #2: June 2020.

Spirit Horse > Chaos: A Poetry Vortex [ Webzine ]: Spring 2020 and Flapper Press [ Website ]: May 28, 2020.

Lone Wolf > Fleas on the Dog #6 [ Webzine ]: Spring 2020.

Barren > Poetry X Hunger [ Website ]: May 10, 2020 and North of Oxford #5 [ The Pandemic Issue ] [ Webzine ]: August 11, 2020.

Masques Up > North of Oxford #5 [ The Pandemic Issue ]: August 11, 2020

Moving Game > Words and Whispers [ Webzine ] #1: Fall 2020 [ Black Lives Matter Section ].

The Fallen > Musings During a Time of Pandemic [ Anthology ]: Kistrech Theatre International, 2020.

Proper Burial > Black Lives Matter 2020: Vol. 1 [ Anthology ]: Moonstone Press, 2020.

Piccolo Orso > Best Poetry Online [ Website ]: July 1, 2020, Benicia Herald [ Newspaper ]: August 5, 2020 [ in the column Going The Distance ] and Musings During a Time of Pandemic: Kistrech Theatre International, 2020.

Oathsworn > Best Poetry Online : July 1, 2020.

Out Front > North of Oxford #5 [ The Pandemic Issue ]: August 11, 2020 and Benicia Herald [ Newspaper ]: August 23, 2020.

Samaritan > Brickplight [ Webzine ]: Fall 2020, Geography is Irrelevant [ Anthology ]: Stairwell Press, 2020 and Lion and Lilac [ Webzine ]: December 1, 2020.

Whine > Otherwise Engaged [ Magazine ] #6: Winter 2020.

Slavestate > Brickplight: Fall 2020 and Lion and Lilac: December 1, 2020.

Not the Time > Brickplight: Fall 2020 and Lion and Lilac: December 1, 2020.

Spoken > The Writers and Readers Magazine: January-February 2021 and Glimpse [ Magazine ] #54: Fall 2021.

Duck Hill > Poetry Superhighway [ Website ]: November 28, 2020.

The Mystery Ends > Nzuri: Journal of Coastline College
[ Webzine ]: November 11, 2020.

Precipice > Boundless: The Anthology of the Rio Grande Valley
International Poetry Festival: Flower Song Press, 2021.

Bro Way > The Phare [ Webzine ]: November – December 2020,
Scissortail Quarterly [ Magazine ] #1: November 2020, Glimpse
#53: Spring 2021 and Dyst #4: January 2021.

Precipice > Otherwise Engaged #6: Winter 2020, Flapper Press
[ Website ]: December 31, 2020 and Red Skies: A Creator's
Response to 2020 [ Anthology ]: Splintered Disorder Press, 2021.

Rolling Out > Otherwise Engaged #6: Winter 2020 and Waxy &
Poetic: 100 Days, 100 Poems of What's Next [ Website ]: January
31, 2021.

Five Word Challenge > Waxy & Poetic: 100 Days, 100 Poems of
What's Next: January 21, 2021.

In Three Stanzas > Wordcity Monthly [ Webzine ] #5: January
2021, The Writers and Readers Magazine: January-February
2021 and The Poeming Pigeon: From Pandemic to Protest
[ Anthology ]: 2021.

Anti-Social Network > Beliveau Review [ Magazine ] #4: Spring
2021.

Fragment 2019 > The Writers Club [ Website ] [ Writing Gallery
section ]: April 24, 2021.

Pretty > Mocking Owl Roost [ Magazine ] Volume 4, #1:
Community > Fall 2021.

Iola > Rising Phoenix Review [ Webzine ]: May 7, 2021 and
Decolonial Passage [ Webzine ]: September 18, 2021.

Pretty > Decolonial Passage: September 18, 2021.

In Three Stanzas > Reimagine America [ Anthology ]: Vagabond,
2022.

# ABOUT THE AUTHOR

Dee Allen. is an African-Italian performance poet based in Oakland, California. Active on the creative writing & Spoken Word tips since the early 1990s. Author of 5 books, *Boneyard, Unwritten Law, Stormwater and Skeletal Black*, all from POOR Press, and from Conviction 2 Change Publishing, *Elohi Unitsi*, his first in both traditional print and digital versions, and 36 anthology appearances under his figurative belt so far. *Rusty Gallows* is Allen's 6th book to date.

VAGABOND

# PRAISE FOR RUSTY GALLOWS

"With *Rusty Gallows: Passages Against Hate*, Dee Allen. continues his work as an alert witness to our times. Rooted in a common history and collective grievous past, Allen evokes the radical Dr. King and fuses the dream to contemporary headlines while offering an appreciation for every waking day. An alive, time transcendent collection for anyone seeking truth and a world where people prevail over profit, where racism and war are not the answer, and a room of one's own is a human right instead of a luxury, Allen's words point the direction home."

~ Denise Sullivan, San Francisco Examiner

Dee Allen's "Rusty Gallows: Passage Against Hate" is a history-filled primer for how to live in a post-white supremacist world. His masterful flow of words etch deep grooves of oppression, genocide, lynchings, but also humor and inclusiveness. It's a multi-cultural examination of the horrors of white-on-top, including lynchings of Italians, scenes from the Native American genocide, and murders in churches, mosques and synagogues. Yet, he implores us to come together with song lyrics that are suitable for the next set of rallies. This voice is vital in a time of widening polarity. "Rusty Gallows" cries for a multi-cultural community of solutions. It will be re-read for its important lessons.

~ Doug Stuber, edits *Poems from the Heron Clan* [ Magazine ]

**www.vagabondbooks.net**